think of
the world
as a
mirror maze

More praise for:
Think of the World as a Mirror Maze

Caitlin Vance's *Think of the World as a Mirror Maze* is the antidote to the apocryphal stories about women the culture wants us to believe. No sugar and spice, no Miss Manners, no cleaving unto a man. Instead, on these pages, Vance paints vivid, sometimes bloody, and always mesmerizing images of a striving toward a truer, fiercer sense of the feminine, or at times, more pointedly, images of how that fierceness is contained and repressed: "My mother's skin is stretched on the hunter's wall/like a canvas left to dry." The speakers in Vance's poems make clear they are not going to end up stretched across someone's wall. They may just be the hunter and not the hunted. Their smiles are: "made of small, sharp bones/meant to rip/the flesh of a dumber animal." As the speaker in the final poem says, "The sun can do whatever it wants/and, I realize suddenly, so can I." And in this book, Vance does whatever she wants, bravely and without regard for what anyone thinks she should do.

—Christopher Kennedy, Author of
Clues from the Animal Kingdom

'Everyone thinks you're sweet / but you're not.' So ends the first poem in this disarming debut, a collection that combines a surrealist's wildness with a realist's keen observation to arrive at insights so psychologically precise you'll see that even if you think you're sweet, there are a number of ways you're not. These are poems populated by many selves, shadows, strangers, by a loathed pet rat and a horse on fire in the middle of a street, by a mother and father also flailing, sometimes asserting, 'The dead have to listen to the living,' and sometimes whispering, 'Jesus probably isn't real, but let's pretend he is, just in case.' This is a book that seems always in the third person, even when a poem is written in the first or second, meaning Caitlin Vance is a poet who understands the powers of character, story, and point of view. If these speaker-characters are not sweet, they are still very much tender. What they understand is that real tenderness, however surreally inhabited, requires real risk. Dreams have consequences—you may not die in them, but they can jab you into seeing the life you've been living, and then the life you're hungry for.

—Chen Chen, Author of *When I Grow Up
I Want to Be a List of Further Possibilities*

think of the world as a mirror maze

poems by
caitlin vance

Stubborn Mule Press
Devil's Elbow, MO
stubbornmulepress.com

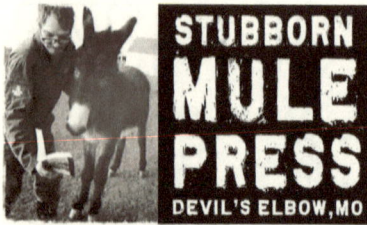

All poems copyright © Caitlin Vance 2019

First Edition 11 7 5 3 2 1
ISBN: 978-1-950380-29-9
LCCN: 2019939507
Design, edits and layout: Jeanette Powers
stubbornmulepress@gmail.com @stubbornmulepress
Cover Image: Jon Lee Grafton
Interior Photo: Caitlin Vance
Bio Photo: Monica Albu

Are you really reading this? Congratulations, we love you. No one but the author can really claim rights to their work, no matter what law says what. And we can't really do anything about theft, whatever that means, so here is our pact: Be cool, be kind, don't steal, email the author if you like or want to riff off their work. Also, let us at Stubborn Mule know if you want to write a review, we'll share it and your review publication, too. Go ahead and use passages for reviews, accolades, or epigraphs, give credit where credit is due. Let's stay radical, share with us our honor among anarchists.

Enormous thanks to Stubborn Mule Press and editor Jeanette Powers for publishing *Think of the World as a Mirror Maze*. Thank you to Jon Lee Grafton for the beautiful cover art, and to Monica Albu for the author photo.

Thank you to the English & Creative Writing departments at Colby College, Syracuse University, and the University of Louisiana at Lafayette for supporting me in my creative and intellectual journeys.

Thanks to all my teachers. Special thanks to Christopher Kennedy, Bruce Smith, Brooks Haxton, Mary Karr, Debra Spark, Peter Harris, Natalie Harris, Adrian Blevins, Patrick Donnelly, Skip Fox, and Sadie Hoagland.

Thanks to all my friends, classmates, and others who have supported my writing and given me feedback on some of the poems in this book. Special thanks to Brent Daly, Jess Acosta, David Gustavson, Casey Nagle, Tina Johnson, Chen Chen, Becca Shaw Glaser, Erin J. Mullikin, Jess Poli, Jessica Scicchitano, Cate McLaughlin, Patrick Dundon, Grant Patch, and Nicole Ziemlak.

Thank you also to my mother, sister, father, and stepmother.

Specialest thanks to Michael Keen, Desmond, and Mei.

table of contents

I
Dream Poem About Matricide...13
The Older Girl..15
In Your Neighbor's Front Yard..16
Letter of Complaint to a Dead Grandfather.................................17
Lights...18
A Mother Is a Vase Falling...19
A Young Deer Wanders Into a Hunter's House...........................20
My First Vision...21
Survival Skills From My Father..22
Survival Skills From My Mother...24

II
In Your High School Dream...26
My Relationship with Beauty Will Always Be Conflicted............27
What My Father Said to Me This Morning.................................29
Love Poem About My Internalized Homophobia,
     Which I Learned at Church..30
Blood Comes Like Rain After a Drought:
     Poem in Response to Your Shitty Poem..........................31
I Used to Play a Game Called Whiskey Slaps.............................33
Sad Love Poem...35
In Your Christmas Dream..38
Love Poem in Which I Lose (on Christmas), But So Do You....39
Valentine's Day at the Psych Ward..40
Evening with Little Comfort..41
Survival Skills from My Hypothetical Child...............................42

III
No One Is In Trouble But You..44
Smile...45
Love Poem in Which I Lose (to a Killer)...................................46
Upon Receiving a Small Inheritance from My Dead Mother...50
When the Neighbors Get Evicted..51

What I Told My Daughter About the Sun..................................52
Northern Winters..54
The Wedding Picture..55
Winter Landscape After Betrayal...56
Survival Skills from My Sister...57
Survival Skills from My Daughter's Barbie Doll.......................59
April...60

Author's Note:

This is a work of poetry, not a work of nonfiction. One neat thing about poetry (as I see it) is that it doesn't have to be "true," but it doesn't have to be "not true," either. However, readers often do read poetry as if it were nonfiction, as if the author of the poem and the speaker (or narrator) of the poem are the same person, as if all events portrayed are true and as if all sentiments that seem to be felt by the speaker are also felt by the poet in real life. While some poetry may function this way, mine often does not. Some of these poems are inspired by real events, but even in those works I have taken liberties to alter both material facts and emotional realities. Other poems are based on dreams or just my imagination and bear little resemblance to "reality" at all. This is all to say that if you read this work as nonfiction, you will pick up inaccurate "facts." This book does not offer facts, only fragments of emotion obscured through the mirror maze.

Let this note also serve as a content warning/trigger warning to readers. This book contains description and discussion of sexual assault, sexual violence, suicidality, mental illness, and other potentially upsetting topics.

Caitlin Vance
2019

Dream Poem About Matricide

Two women identical to your mother
stand in the doorway of your room.
A strange man—maybe God, maybe

Satan, says
*one is your real mother,
the other an imposter.*

Both women smile at you
with teeth,
not how your shy mother
usually smiles—

mouth closed and eyes
blank as a chalkboard.
You must make your best guess—

one will own you,
the other will die.

If you choose wrong
the evil mother will knife
out small pieces
of your heart and brain
each day and slowly
through her smiling mouth

she'll take all of you into
herself. Of course
you point to the way of darkness

and your real mother fades
from this world
quiet as a scream
reaching for you
till she's dust.

While your new mother sleeps,

you open her red throat
with your bare hands,

peel a string of her
vocal chords,
staple her voice to your own.

Everyone thinks you're sweet
but you're not.

The Older Girl

When I was six an older girl came to live with us.
I never learned for sure if she was human
or a ghost. She could have been an exchange student.
She had skirts made of paper and hair that held the wind
and made low moans of harpsichords. Crow feathers hung
from her ears. She'd glide alone through crowds

in our city. She said streets filled with strangers freed her.
Instead of swallowing herself, pushing in and under
like eyeballs in meditation, she could just exist.
She'd walk to a nearby hill and smoke. Instead of sneaking out
between her teeth, the smoke hid inside the toy trunk
of her chest. She thought we wouldn't know, but I could see

through her skin. The crow feathers singed at the ends
like scraps of paper floating and slowly burning in the wind.
Once I followed her to the top of the hill and hid
under the bench. She had miniature doors in her pocket that day
and she lined them up in the dirt, one after the other.
She took out a tiny doll and stuck him in the front. All the doors

were open with ants crawling through them, except the last,
which was stuck. The doll threw his arms at the sky and howled
like a seagull flying far out over the ocean to greet death. The girl
did the same. The doll and the doors vanished with a November wind
and so did she. She left those crow feathers behind, which sit
in my palms, sparking even now.

In Your Neighbor's Front Yard

You know the neighbor's cat hides in the rain forest of ferns
so you crawl inside to find her. Space expands.
A parrot song rustles in the wind
and wild lizards dance beside your feet.
Red dust falls off the backs of ferns
and coats the giant forest's floor, a red carpet.

The cat is a single lion rebelling from the pride
and you're a poacher.
You spy on her, twenty feet away
through the window-shade gaps of a large fern.
The lion grooms herself on a rock.

You decide you are no longer a poacher,
but a friend.

You sneak up to pet her
but when she sees you she growls,
bites, runs away.
Reaching down from the canopy,
a giant hand

lifts you up through the forest's canopy.
It's the neighbor boy,
too old and tall for the forest
and now you're in his arms.
He has been eating a banana
and smashes the remains into your nose.
He takes a few steps,
puts you down in some gravel,

and goes away.
You brush the fruit and germs off your face.
You spread your hands across your eyes,
look through the gaps between your fingers like window-shades.

Letter of Complaint to a Dead Grandfather

You gave me a pet rat for my third birthday. I hated that rat
because it was ugly and grey and a boy, but my mother said
I had to keep it and even write you thank-you notes
on my Rainbow Brite stationary. She didn't understand. That rat lived

for ages. You had been smudged at the edges with an eraser.
You never spoke and I never spoke and you made me shy
forever. You taught me to tuck my secrets in the dust
between two notebook pages, and to put that notebook under my bed
with the spider webs. Or better yet, into the flames. Years later

at your military funeral in rural Washington, my mother
made me bring the rat on my shoulder. There were girls
with Coach purses I'd never seen before, and girls
with faces stretched and shadowed by meth I'd seen everywhere.
While the soldiers stood in straight lines folding flags and shooting guns

I thought about that time when my sister, as a toddler,
shoved a long green tinker toy into your eyeball
which was yellow like the pages of an old book.

There was a reception at the Camano Island Community Center.
You told me Camano Island was not an island, but it is.
You never lived there. None of the middle-aged women
with glittering eyelids and ponytails knew you.
I sat with Ray, a trucker who stared rudely at the rat
and ate my pie when it was clear I wouldn't.
Ray didn't seem to have known you either. You were dead

but I still had this rat, and I still had to sit, waiting,
in green rainy nowhere until I shed enough guilt to leave.
Your rat still sat perched on my shoulder for some years after that,
always gnawing on my scarves. Then one hot night

in a motel in Oregon, he lashed at the red Christmas lights beneath
my cheeks. That was the last I could take,
so I made everyone watch as
I crushed him between two pages of a notebook
and put it all into the flames.

Lights

The boys gather in the center of the cul de sac
looking for something to do. They are twelve
and it's night. Under the streetlights everything is wet
from rain—black roads, green-black leaves,
wings of roadkill. One boy gets an idea. The children

cut a piece of cardboard into the shape of a cat,
use tinfoil to give her reflecting eyes.
They place the cat in the middle of the road
lined on either side by a thick layer of trees.
When a car approaches, its driver will slam
on the breaks, potentially sliding off the road

into a tree, perhaps causing thousands of dollars
worth of damage to the car and the bodies
inside. Some other child
who belongs to the driver
will not receive a birthday present. The boys wait
in the trees, quivering, covering their mouths
to keep from laughing

or making any sound. Their eyes flicker
at each other like fireflies,
shining demons. One boy thinks
of saying something like *Hey, let's go home,
and let's take that cat thing with us,*
but he doesn't. Another boy
thinks of saying something too.
Their hearts are hot,
their clothes are damp, their minds are aflame.
Their eyes flicker at each other like headlights.

A Mother is a Vase Falling

It's been sixteen years and she hasn't had a date.
It's too late for that, she says,
as if she won't live another thirty years

at least. As someone who has lived only sixteen years,
I don't understand why people think life is over at fifty-five,
or seventy-seven, or when they become mothers.
I'd like to say something about flowers,
but she has none. She has trees.

Usually when she's home she's watching TV, but once
I saw her lying on the floor with two cans of soup.
She said she was exercising. Later I held the soup
in my hands, cursing her for not knowing
who Warhol was. Craving tomatoes,
I cooked the soup, nicking her torn-up heart

as well as mine. A mother is a vase
falling. Or, if you prefer, she's an artist's pencil
in the lightest shade, which is made of the hardest
graphite. You have to press like hell
to make a mark. A mother is a vase falling,

but not breaking. She's put in some good carpet.
This doesn't mean I won't be back tomorrow,
same as before, brushing my careless sleeves
against her bruises.

A Young Deer Wanders Into a Hunter's House

My mother's skin is stretched on the hunter's wall
like a canvas left to dry. I am small
and my shadow, red
for some reason, wanders across the skin
as if looking for its way home. The shadow
sniffs the air for something familiar.
It does what I do not.

I'll be damned if my own skin appears stretched
like a canvas someday. My grandmother's skin
is stretched on the wall, too.
She is smaller than my mother
and on her skin is not my singular, life-size shadow
but a hundred tiny ones,

each the size of a hornet. They run
towards the skin's edge
but they are running in place. How many generations
of female ancestors do I have? The wind comes

and washes them away
but they come back
like a tide,

like the sun each morning.
I see a video of myself on the wall,
not a shadow this time, and I wander
through the woods, lost.
I cannot find the edge

of the screen, the end of the forest.
Snow falls all around me.
I act like I don't notice it.
The flakes are like bullets
that can't touch me.
Or maybe they're just shadows.

My First Vision

I'm not sure why I saw them. I was having a fine day,
if a bit boring. My brother the boy scout
had built a small wooden car and today was the race

against the rest of the scouts. In the high school gym
parents circled the perimeter of the race track
and snapped photos or held signs shouting *Go Ryan!*
Go Phil! I was a girl

and I found another girl there—another sister
of one of the scouts. We went outside. The light was pink

or orange or lavender, as it is just before dark.
We pretended we had cars of our own, real cars
roaring through the courtyard where we'd eat lunch
years later as freshmen. Then I saw them: a dozen male

construction workers with orange hats and shirts that said
Go Phil!, climbing ladders into the sky. I called out
to them. They wouldn't answer. One looked at me
as if to say, *There's nothing to explain here.*

We're working, and you're a little girl. I pointed
the men out to my friend. She couldn't see them,

but she believed me that they were there.
That's the good thing about other girls.
They believe you.

Survival Skills from My Father

You were born with the umbilical cord wrapped around your neck, so I knew you'd be special.

Send positive energy out into the universe, and good things will come back to you. If something bad happens, you weren't sending out enough positive energy.

When the bad man's ghost tries to choke you in the night, set some herbs on fire by your bed.

When he's still there say to him *By universal law, I demand that you leave.* The dead have to listen to the living.

To protect those you love, instead of praying at night, imagine each of your loved ones, circle their bodies in light.

Think of the world as a mirror maze, the kind at a carnival.

You're not hallucinating, you just see things other people can't.

Don't listen to your mother.

Jesus only wants your money.

When I was five I knew my neighbor's son would die in a car crash, so I told her this. Then he *really* died, the next day. I was scared.

You're the same as me, but don't be scared.

Women are taught to be perfect, but you can only be *so* perfect. I don't want you to be perfect.

You don't remember, but before you were born you chose me to be your father, based on the lessons you needed to learn in this life. When it's over you'll go through the cycle again, until you've learned everything there is to know. Then you'll become part of the sky, sleep in stardust.

Now you have my last name.

The bad man's ghost is standing right behind you. He says *hello*. What do you say?

Survival Skills from My Mother

If you practice enough, you won't even need to look in a mirror to put on your makeup.

Jesus probably isn't real, but let's pretend he is, just in case.

You *are* hallucinating, but that's just how you are.

When you don't exercise I can see the nervous energy rising in you like steam.

Life is not a Hallmark card. Jesus knows this; he made it this way.

Heaven is an exclusive nightclub with the lights turned on too harsh. And there's no smoking or one-night stands.

Birth control ruins your mood, your sex drive, and your body. They've been working on birth control for men since I was young, but men complained too much about the same side effects we've had to deal with from the beginning. Men are trash. Condoms are the best option.

If a man buys you a six-dollar drink, this doesn't mean you have to sleep with him, even though he'll make you feel that way. But six dollars? Come on.

Ghosts are not real, and the lottery is pointless. You have a higher chance of giving birth to conjoined twins, or being killed by a vending machine. Actual facts.

Yes Walmart is bad, but where else are you going to shop, Whole Foods? How are you going to afford avocados *and* condoms?

You will have to take out loans to pay off credit card debt.

Actually, forget the condoms. If you stick to women you won't need condoms.

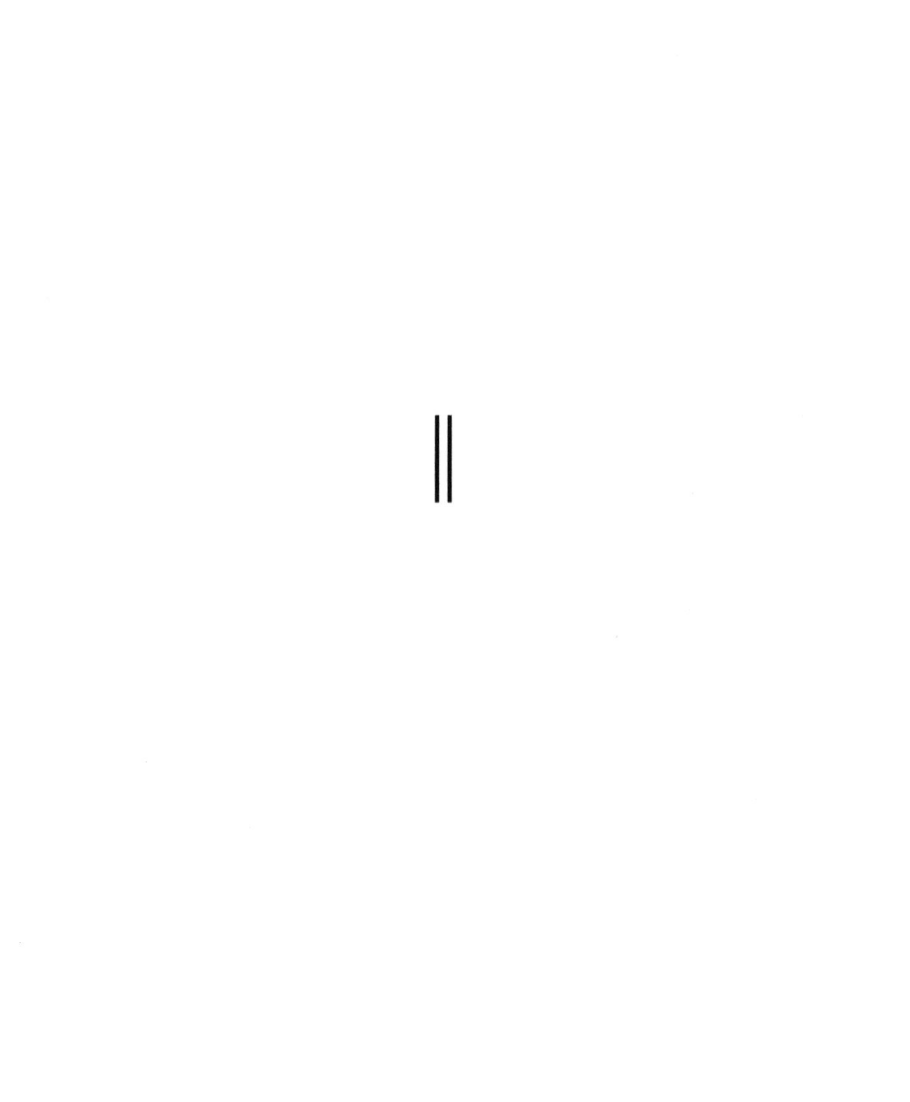

In Your High School Dream

You are pregnant and lost and alone
in a corn field. It is hot.
You're pretty sure you are a virgin.
Something burns inside you and you know it's time.
But you don't know how to deliver a baby

so you grab a piece of corn and shuck it.
Your baby is inside. A second sun rises

in the sky, and several stars
with faces.
Your baby is gone. You want to call his name
but you don't know what it is.
You check your watch, then follow
the sound of a staple gun

into the woods, and you know
it's the football team
beating the new members
with PVC pipes. You hope
and don't hope it's your baby
who has joined
the team. You find a garden of carrots,

pull one out by its hair. It is not a carrot
but the father of your child,
a mascot with a PVC pipe.
You hit him
and take the pipe,
which becomes your baby,
then a carrot,
which you cook in the oven of a tree.

My Relationship With Beauty Will Always Be Conflicted

All my favorite stories begin with a pretty woman
in a photograph. Somewhere, a baby girl has just seen her daddy
for the last time. She won't remember him,
but she'll find a picture
(he is gorgeous too).

I try to convince myself physical beauty is subjective,
it is culturally constructed,
I am a feminist...
But these truths seem only partial.

When I look at the models in magazines
I wonder who broke their hearts,

and I like to watch the ugly man's pretty wife
in an unguarded moment,
looking to her side, sad.

Why do we think sad women are beautiful?
And crazy women and silent women
and French women smoking...

The girl I'm dating is pretty
but she says French women are unfairly beautiful.

I want to look like you,
I want to look better than you,
I want to have sex with you.

I don't want to have sex with you because you look better than me.

I don't want to have sex with you because you look worse than me.
Try harder.

It is undeniable some people are more beautiful than others,
violently so. The pretty woman in the photograph
rips apart the unhappy marriage, and she is ripped apart
in turn. She is fragile, just a photograph. Basically paper,

easiest thing in the world to rip.

The sorority girl leaps off the elliptical machine
and in the bathroom stall later vomits.
Her sisters circled the too-fat parts of her body in black marker,
told her to lose that or lose them.
Have you ever seen a pair of tweezers or a razor blade?

Have you seen those flame shades of lipstick, or a surgeon's knife
cutting under the eyeball of a rich grandmother?

My stepmother, once a pretty woman in a photograph,
used tattoo needles to sew lipstick and eyebrows to her face,
permanently.
In one story, the stepmother tries to kill the stepdaughter
because a talking mirror tells her the stepdaughter is prettier.
How red the apple to remind us of blood.

Have you ever tried to look nice
and then everyone thinks you're asking for it?

The woman doesn't even have to come for a baby to be born.

Have you ever loved someone
who happened to be too beautiful for you?
Or maybe you're unable to love the person you should,
because they're not pretty enough.
I once wanted to be smart but now I prefer beautiful.

Is it possible to be beautiful and not stuck in a photograph?

Maybe stuck in a photograph is easier.
I could follow the advice my mother gave me:

If you're pretty enough, you'll never have to be an adult,
and your husband will take care of you forever

until some young bitch pushes you out of the photograph
and you have to kill her with an apple

which solves nothing anyway
and, besides, is ugly.

What My Father Said to Me This Morning

I'm doing okay. The cats are fine and we
got the furnace fixed and your stepmom's back
doesn't hurt so much today. I wrote you
a letter, only I can't write so I recorded my voice
on a tape. In ten years they won't have tapes—
how weird is that—
that's why I gave you so many extra batteries.

You can listen to this letter once I'm gone,
which will be in only a year and the sooner
you accept it the easier. Already I flash
in and out of this world like light
inside a bulb. It's not that I want to leave you,

you know. It's just that once recently I was at a meeting
and I saw the air split open for me right in front of everyone.
It opened into darkness and I felt I was supposed to leave.
I know this wouldn't make any sense to your sister
but I trust you understand me. When you look at strangers
do you see yourself? I do.

And I love everyone. No,
that doesn't mean I love everything everyone does.
Far from it. I hate everything everyone does. Anyway,
you need to know that I am starting to come and go
like clouds, like moths in your home, like dust
or a chorus or the moon and slow
days in the life of a child.

Love Poem About My Internalized Homophobia, Which I Learned at Church

A beautiful woman has sex with me in what may or may not be hell.
The walls of her apartment are red
and she understands nothing, being drunk again on wine

from the bar downstairs. After she falls asleep
I conduct a hell-themed experiment.
I light big black sugar ants on fire
with matches, which to them are flaming trees.
I've built a model of Dante's circles

on the coffee table, and I assign each of their corpses—
separate the gluttons from the whores
from the traitors. Some float in red rivers of blood
and fire. I staple others together
in a permanent sex.
Dante claims it's winter in the worst circle

and I agree. Satan is a dead bat I stabbed
and stuck in the freezer, his wings now cased in ice.
I wake the woman and ask:
do you want this to happen to you??
To Satan, you are nothing but an ant.
And his wings are cased in ice.

She says she doesn't give a shit about Satan
and I shouldn't worry about myself. She kisses me
and falls back asleep.

But I am alive, and Satan is small
and dead and his wings are melting. I can move
the ants around as I please. The woman is asleep.
Still, I walk downstairs, into the bar,
kiss any
man with a cross around his neck.

Blood Comes Like Rain After a Drought:
Poem in Response to Your Shitty Poem

The one about how you don't like wearing condoms
because you want to feel something *real*
even if it's only *fleeting*, and I'm so *tight*

you just couldn't stop *hitting it* when I asked you to
all those times. You tore the page
out of your journal.

What's real is the fifty-dollar
morning-after pills you can't afford
and neither can I, but guess whose
credit card they end up on? The ghost
of a baby claims my body as its house,

my body is haunted by something no one can see.
Blood comes like rain after a drought

and I use it to paint my face an intimidating red
—*don't even think about being born*—

I imagine my uterus as an inflated heart. Just as red,
just as much blood and a strong muscle
that works automatically,

controlling my body. I am haunted by an infant

or not even, just a spoonful of semen, a tiny cloud
attached to a thought.

At night when I'm alone
and it's dark and nearly silent
except for the sounds of the old house
cracking its arthritic bones,
the part of me that is still a child wonders
if the house is haunted.

It's like that inside my body all the time

but I can't kill that ghost
always watching me,
only she has no eyes, never did,

plus she's inside a tiny cave with no lights

which is also how I imagine my brain
(where I live). I can't stay in this world.
So we're the same, she and I.

I'll never tell you
the name I gave her.

I don't give a fuck how tight I am or how famous you are.

No, you can't not wear a condom,
no, you can't kiss me, no, you can't fuck me, no, you can't
borrow *The Scarlet Letter*.

I'd like to send you a box made of skin
that screams when you cut it open,
and then this baby ghost
will climb inside your body, your rooms,
give you what you deserve.

I Used to Play a Game Called Whiskey Slaps

A long time ago, someone built a wall inside my body. It closes off my lungs from my heart, heart from brain, brain from body, my body from what it touches. It is one wall, but it does many things. I am trying to knock this wall down.

I used to play a game called "whiskey slaps." Someone drinks the whiskey, and I slap them to distract from the taste. They take turns. Less than one in five people agree to play this game.

I always agreed to play. Sometimes I slapped so hard I'd knock the person over. I am a girl.

Narcissism is a survival skill when sometimes life's not easy.

I have a question for myself—it's *my* body; why can't I knock down the wall? Maybe I should ask a doctor. Maybe this is what surgery is for. They'll scrape out pieces of the wall with silver tools.

I was born the year the Berlin Wall fell.

The person who built my wall is dead now. I didn't kill him. I can't ask him how to knock the wall down. I never whiskey-slapped him.

Is it my wall? Is it his?

I ask my mother about the wall. She says she doesn't know what a wall is.

My other question—the wall is inside my body. I can't see inside my body. What does the wall look like? Is it bricks? Barbed wire?

These are questions I didn't wish to ask.

I wonder if other people have walls too: Maybe the little girl down the street. Maybe my mother.

More questions: Am I beautiful? Was he?

I no longer play whiskey slaps. I go to an old friend's wedding. I haven't seen these people in a while, and I receive stares. Do I look better, or worse?

Can other people tell I have this wall?
It occurs to me that I might paint the wall. Do I call it a mural, or graffiti?

The wall is inside my body. I can't look at my own painting.

I am trying to knock down this wall without knocking down myself.

A Meditation on Nutcrackers and the Rich

1.
I'd like to understand your mother's house
in the suburbs, why you hate it so much
with the floor-to-ceiling windows,
the piano no one plays.
This town is full of fake things
and too much money, a store called *The Preppy Pink Pony*
and people who just want boys to play sports,
work in banking, and host dinner parties
where they pay people to walk around with trays
of little dead things that no one will eat
because they have too many calories.
And all the people at those parties may never talk
about anything, and may never know each other
despite all the parties.
I guess I can understand hating a place like this,
hating any place if you grew up in it.

2.
In the house where my mother fed me as a baby—
the house where the boy I liked in high school
punched a wall to mix its white contents
with the cocaine he was selling—the walls decayed
and the lights never worked, or the oven.
Frogs lived there which the lazy cat wouldn't kill
and neither would we.

3.
Your new grown-up apartment in the city is a red cave.
You live in a personal hell now and make too little money.
I know it's hard for you to learn that no money
is just as bad as too much money.
Your parents send you checks but you still hate them.
I've read only a fraction of the literature on your bookshelves,
about rich people cheating on each other
and their empty lives, all the time they have
to think about their fractured souls and their failures
and how love's not real and God's not real

and happiness is fake and the only good thing in life is sex
but not with someone you're married to,
or maybe cocaine is a good thing too or bourbon,
but those things are only fleeting, and suicide is cool
because David Foster Wallace did it
and Virginia Woolf, isn't it poetic
how she walked into the river with stones in her pockets?
Well it's not poetic,
what would have been poetic is if she stayed alive
and wrote some poems.

4.
I wish you'd understand my apartment, where I need love
and God and jokes,
because I don't have the right clothes for parties
or enough laundry detergent to wash them,
but if I went to a party where there was a tray of free dead things
I'd eat all of them because they were free
and I need God
because I can't take any more Hell.

5.
The nutcrackers in your mother's house
have cavities in their chests meant to crack
the shells of walnuts.
But none of these cavities where their hearts would be
have ever seen walnuts.
I placed my finger inside just to check
and pressed the lever, but it failed to crack anything,
my bones too strong for their so-called jaws.
Another fake thing I guess.
I asked your mother about the nutcrackers
but she just said that you and I should never have children because
two people as crazy as us could never raise a healthy child.
Your mother gives me new ideas.
She says I need fish oil and a hundred-dollar yoga mat
and a car with Bluetooth,
she says I need black napkins when I wear black, not white napkins,
I need to go to restaurants where black napkins are available upon request.
The candies by her window are coated with sugar crystals,
so we forget

their gelatin cores, made from the bones of sacrificed horses
or cows or whatever animals they use now.
It says nothing about animals on the package,
so I learned from your vegan sister.
I wish special vegan food was not so expensive
and health was not so expensive.
Remember the guy who puts drywall in the cocaine he sells?
I fear our food is like that.
I wish doctors were what I thought they were when I was young—
told the truth and were not motivated by money.
Last time I went to the dentist she just tried to sell me tooth whitener.
I used to think doctors and police officers and presidents
told the truth and knew the truth
because someone has to take care of things.
I used to think adults took care of things.
They don't.

6.
You say that to the people in your mother's house, you are nothing
but a decoration, like the nutcrackers. I don't respond.
I still don't know what's okay to say and what's not.
If I were smarter
and knew the Greek myths and Bible stories
they reference in your literature,
I could talk forever
and maybe heal everyone for free.

In Your Christmas Dream

A horse catches fire in the middle of the street.
You're on your way to buy eggs
for your grandmother. The horse screams like a woman
being murdered with a knife and they load him
into an ambulance. Everyone watches from their lawns.
Dogs, cats, and other horses rush towards
the fire-horse like magnets. You never knew

there were so many horses here.
Cars and bicycles also scream
and run like animals. The ambulance revs its engine.

The animals and cars chase after it.
A stampede of lost minds.
Or gained minds. You have to run
through neighbors' yards to avoid being hit, and you worry
about invading privacy and trampling flowers.
But there are no flowers—

this is Christmas, you suddenly remember. You run
until you reach your grandmother's house—
the one with tiny candles burning
in the windows. You burst in

and are greeted by your grandfather, who has been dead
for years. You embrace
and tears roll down your cheeks.
He asks why you are crying. *Grandpa,* you say,
looking down at your empty hands,
I forgot the eggs.

Love Poem in Which I Lose (on Christmas), But So Do You

I lean over the railing of your mother's balcony
to see the head-shaped dent in the frosty ground,
thirty feet below. It seems too small to explain

your broken back, neck, mind, mouth of shattered teeth,
too broken to speak clearly. I'll never eat again,
having just fled the hospital where you're holding

your breath, still trying to die. It won't work.
Something automatic takes over,
though the skin rips
when faced with a kitchen knife or even paper
carelessly touched. Bones crack like twigs

under a boot. Our hearts are baby animals
frantically throbbing. But you're still alive.
Murder seems easier.
Maybe suicide's like trying to tickle yourself.
Unlike you,

I can't afford to attempt suicide
and fuck it up—
I could jump too, but I walk

down to the ground. I lower my head as if in prayer,
rest it in the dent your head made.
They say the dead souls of real suicides stay
sad forever. Maybe your soul is dead now

inside your living body.
I clasp my hands around my head
in preparation for a headstand.
But my hands won't fit in the hole.

I tell your mother about the head-shaped dent.
She doesn't want to see it.

I fill in the hole with dirt.

Valentine's Day at the Psych Ward

I'm late again for visiting hour and they check my purse
for sharps and cords. You're calm, pumped full
of stabilizers and the quiet you need to heal. You've won
a stuffed bear at Bingo.

Other patients smile at me like
always, because they love me like you do, or rather you
love me like they do—like you'd love an old cartoon

or a Christmas song. I want you to love
me like a wolf loves a pretty deer's
thigh, with teeth, warm blood

in red snow. While you squeeze the bear
I try to remember a time when you did this.
I put on the lipstick I carry in my purse, and I kiss

the bear's forehead at hour's end.
I do not kiss you. You don't seem to notice.

Evening With Little Comfort

8 p.m. and an even-ing out of the world's darkness
    I'd like to escape. I take comfort in headlights,

phone screens, a busy lawyer's lamp still on
    through the office window. Small resistances

to night's tyranny. I take comfort in a heavy glass
    filled with ice which catches glimmers of light

like wedding rings. There's comfort in walking down the sidewalk
    where matches flicker and last season's tinsel hangs

on tree branches in a shop window, there's comfort
    in the glitter painted on the eyelids of a drunk woman

and the voices of strangers saying *look at that moon*.
    At home I lure a firefly in through my window.

My green-eyed cat chases it and scrapes her teeth
    against its little light bulb tail, so all that's left

to flicker are her eyes and mine and not
    the firefly's tiny dead eyes, gone dark.

My cat goes to sleep. I climb into bed, lower
    my eyelids, burn out my last little lamps, surrender.

Survival Skills from My Hypothetical Child

I am an idea inside your mind, and you already love me. In this way, I exist. The only choice you have to make is whether or not to give me a body.

Please don't give me a body unless the world is good, unless you—Mom—are good. I'm quite content inside your mind.

You've always thought of your mind as a cave, and so it is one. A cave is like a womb. I live here, playing with the bear you gave me, loving you back.

When you're scared of the world, you shrink yourself and climb inside. You let me hold you in my arms, with the bear.

Not the kind of cave with a puppet show, the puppet shadows dancing on the wall. But I can perform one for you, if you want.

A hug is just a soft chain.

No One is in Trouble But You

An old friend calls and says, "Beware the sound
of a crying baby left outside
in the night. His wails will climb
through the tiny holes in your window screen
but don't be tricked. It's a grown man
imitating a baby's cry."

"A male siren,"
My old friend says.
"No one
is in trouble
but you."

I can't help but think this is some kind of metaphor—

the animal draw of a child,
the terror that awaits
if I follow it,
someone else telling me what to do.

Smile

A smile
is a sign of happiness
made of small,
sharp bones

meant to rip
the flesh of a dumber animal
to pieces
until it's dead.

Love Poem in Which I Lose (to a Killer)

Do you wonder what I'd look like dead,
do you wonder what my blood tastes like, or how it would feel
to stick a knife in my heart
and turn it like a doorknob,
hear the way I moan for the last time?

You won't tell me how many when I ask
what's your number

but you call me *sweetie*—
nobody is just a killer,
nobody is only one thing.

Before sleeping together we hold hands for weeks
like school children. Nobody waits this long.
It's like you don't live
inside your body.
You cook dead things for me
and we fall asleep in your twin bed
still dressed with a camo blanket.
Sweetie, are you comfortable?

And in the morning you finally pull me onto you
by my scarf which is wrapped
around my neck like a noose.

You don't have any condoms so we don't do it that way.
Killers don't keep condoms in the house.
You haven't done this in a while
so I ask if you're okay a dozen times.
Yes, yes,
thank you sweetie.

So many years after you were eighteen in the Middle East,
killing some motherfuckers,
you still see bodies as *bodies*.
Sex is still too close to death.
Anything involving *bodies* is too close to death.

You were already a killer
when I was an eighth grader with braces
bleeding from a place of sex for the first time.
A boy asked me on a date as a joke
while the pretty girls laughed in the background
in Home Ec class, in suburbia.

You threw bodies into the ground
under the screaming desert sun,
played with the bodies just to be a dick,
smiled and high-fived the other Americans still alive.

Killing's all you ever wanted to do
but now you regret it in your dreams,
you say I make you regret it,
my poems even make you regret it.

Pieces of dead bodies make good weapons in a pinch.
A leg is heavier than it looks
and can be used as a club
(maybe my leg).

What's the sharpest organ?

Time heals all wounds,
but time's not enough.
You have to do the work.

You won't eat but one meal a day now,
just to survive.

I want you in a million ways, not just sexually.

Is one of those ways to rip my leg off
and use it to kill a foreign teenager, maybe a virgin?

Is one of those ways to peer through binoculars
from where I can't see you
and shoot me through my head,
high five the man next to you,
do things to my dead body just to be a dick?

Is one of those ways to rip my lips off with your teeth
and swallow
my blood like a shot?

I hope so.
I don't care what you want
as long as you want.

But I care
when you want only yourself
alone in the woods with no other bodies
except for animals you'll kill
and eat and not fuck, forever.

I've never killed but I worry
there is no way to kill and not go crazy,
there is no way to kill
and not be a different person every day.
Maybe you're a piece of each of those lives you *took*,
maybe you literally took them.

How many hearts have you broken literally?
How many have you broken metaphorically?
Does it still give you pleasure either way?
Don't lie.

"Broken heart" is a dead metaphor.
That means we forget.
You think I'm sweet,

but I wonder what you'd look like dead too.
That's what love is this time.

I want a knight's armor
and to sword fight someone who won't kill me
when I lose.
Well you didn't lose.
Breaking hearts must be easy for killers,
easy as a doorknob.

It's like I'm in love with myself.

I don't know why.

I don't want to know why.

Sweetie,
it ain't nothing.

Upon Receiving a Small Inheritance From My Dead Mother

I buy a piano from the pawn shop.
She always wanted to learn. I buy some flower seeds,
pink paint for the living room.
The paint turns the walls a muted shade
of her blood. I saw her blood.
The walls are like a crime scene photograph

blurred by time and sun. I return
to the store and buy a light shade of blue
but after re-painting the walls are still a muted shade

of her blood, pre-death, when I could still see it
in the veins beneath the skin of her wrists.
I have a little money left
but I won't waste it on more paint. It occurs to me

I am dispensing what is left of my mother,
a number dwindling on a computer screen.
The piano sits untouched in the blue room. I try
to sell it back—they'll give me half
what I paid. I'll have half my mother back,

just eighty pounds of her,
black and white keys for teeth,
sitting in the corner of the blue room.
I go home. I can't play the piano.
I turn the radio on instead.

When the Neighbors Get Evicted

A ghost moves in, boards up all the windows.
She lets no one inside except for me. She offers me water
and when she opens her mouth to drink
a light in her throat shines out

like a moon-ray. A wound breathes in the side of her head
where the bullet hit. *The scars I had while living are gone,*
she says. *Only this remains, the one that killed me.*
A sound emanates from her wound,

a faint screech like the music of a novice violin player.
She says she'll never leave this place. She braids my hair
but I can't braid hers. She says the reason she died at thirty
was her inability to tell a lie. Is it possible

to pinpoint the moment you fall in love?
I wonder if love is just envy, sometimes. The closest thing to light
in my own throat is the shine of saliva. And that only shows
when the light of her throat illuminates mine.

We can't have sex or marry, but she moves in with me,
into my rooms and my mind. I always thought the mind
was a room, a cave with windows. She holds my head in her hands,
braids my hair, braids the curtains of my mind-windows,

pushes them aside so the light in her throat
can shine through.

What I Told My Daughter About the Sun

It is not God, nor is it electronic.
The sun is hotter than any fire you'll ever see.
It could chew and swallow one million Earths

and while you sleep it flies across the world
to visit people you'll never meet.
It climbs through their windows
during their last moments of slumber,
slow and careful like a cat

or an intruder. It warms their rooms,
burns their cheeks a bit
if they lay there too long.
The sun rises in the east and sets in the west.
When the sun sets here in California
it dips under the ocean—can you hear it

hissing? It sleeps with cold whales until morning
when it rises from underground somewhere east.
Don't ask me how it gets there.

In New York the sun sets into the ground and rises
out of the ocean, yawning and picking seaweed

out of its teeth. When the sun lights your path
from the bus stop to your door it keeps you safe.

But don't stand under it too long.
It will give you cancer.

And the tiny puddles of your eyes
are no match for the sun—if you stare
your eyes will burn and burn out,

and it will be dark for you forever

though the sun will still live, cold
and dark, in your mind.

And eventually,
the sun *will* consume the Earth.

There's no way around it.
Let's just hope
you'll be dead before that happens.

Northern Winters

The world is a series of chandeliers.
Little lost animals turn to ice,
then glass, black stone. The lights dim
inside our minds. I always thought the mind was a cave

or a room, a twilit study
with votive candles and endless shelves
and the clean head of a moose.
Pages flip and strangers pass silently
through the door. Out the window
we see icicles and snowflakes—
we can't decide if we want to be still

or aimlessly adrift.
We treat the strangers however we want,
offering them a warm bed, or tea
with poison. We want

to wreck things. So we pray
to the quiet pink sky to turn us, also,
to ice, so we can be still

and then melt and come back
as April rain. But ice washes the mind
like bleach through a drain. And the thaw
leaves us a clearing, where old grey leaves
scrape a badly-swept floor.

The Wedding Picture

When he left he took nothing,
so the wedding picture stayed
in their closet. Now her closet. The picture stayed,
like all things that had become *theirs*:
bedsheets, coffee maker, wedding gift
bird bath. He took only what was *his*—
some clothes and books—as if this
were considerate. She wanted to burn what was theirs

and she might have
if it weren't for the children.
The bird bath belonged to the couple
and the children and the birds.
She was no longer part of the couple.
It was not hers to burn.

She let the children weave through everything:
the bird bath in the yard, the bed sheets,
the closet. It wasn't fair

he left it all here.
And the kids.

In her dreams she burned them to a crisp.

Winter Landscape After Betrayal

A meadow. The edges of the sky curling
like the edges of damp paper. Yellow leaking off the edges
like watercolor. The smell of cigarettes
wafting off a woman's jacket—breaking glass.
Wolves. Wolves ripping dead meat off the bone.
A wheelbarrow and carving into wet cement
in July. A bat in the New England house, locked in a room.
I'm not supposed to enter the room for fear
of rabies. But I do, and I find no bat. A child saying,
*love is words breaking apart like eggshells. It's names
growing stronger.* Me, biting my lip at the front of the classroom.
Everyone else in the world asleep. You saying
not the branch, but the space around it.
The screech of a train. Mountains. Marbles
in the grandfather's pocket, knocking,
making the animals wonder. Mascara from days ago
still waxed onto eyelashes, so much shorter than they were before.
Snipping them off with scissors. Snipping them off with wire cutters.
Electrical fire. Every sheet of paper you ever touched nailed
to my walls. Nailed to my nails. I can't open doors
or eat with forks. Thousands of dead butterflies in glass cases.
Cat's feet on the cases. Cat's feet on my eyelids.
The filling of holes with gasoline. The lighting of a match.
The first firefly anyone has ever seen. Feeling my own hands
catch the firefly and squish it, to my horror, and flick it in the mud.
An empty prayer house in the woods in a foreign country.
The statue of Buddha that lives in my pocket,
shattered. The pieces drifting out to sea.
Me drifting out to sea. Organs floating out of my body,
suspended in water. Losing the brain, losing the lungs.
Water rushing into the lungs, which float
apart from me. Fish biting them. The lungs choking.
God saying, *you must stitch the pieces, you must stitch them
with thread or seaweed or the strands of your own hair.*

Survival Skills from My Sister

The body positive movement is not for everyone.

Don't buy things you can't afford. This will be easier if you have no children.

If you really think crystals are magic, you're a moron. Astrology's not real either, or Jesus.

You should take some meds for those hallucinations.

Most people never find happiness, but the best way to get through life is to avoid mirrors, sad songs, and Jesus.

You're never too old to drink the dumb alcohols, like flavored vodka.

Stop trying to get our parents to understand you.

Polyamory only works about 5% of the time, but monogamy works about 1% of the time.

You're too queer to live anywhere but the Pacific Northwest.

The positive energy stuff leads to victim-blaming. The Law of Attraction is inherently anti-feminist.

Capitalism ruined everything, but it's what we have to work with. The only lucrative career choice is computer programming. You don't need to read T. S. Eliot to do this.

Don't do psychedelics. The ideas they give you sprout in your brain like invasive species. And do *not* listen to sad songs on psychedelics.

Painting your nails is pointless. This will only attract straight women.

It's sad, but if you cheat before your partner does, you're the one in power. But this will draw you to mirrors. You don't want that.

Grandma sewed clothes for Barbie dolls, then gave them to charity. Poor kids don't need Barbie dolls. They ruin your life. They draw you to mirrors.

Survival Skills from My Daughter's Barbie Doll

Let a child tell you what clothes look best on your body. Children are forgiving, but they do not lie.

I'm sure you've heard the proportions of my body are off—my waist too small, my chest too big. If I were human, I wouldn't be able to stand or hold my head up. I wouldn't be able to walk.

But I'm not human.

Some humans get plastic surgery to look like me. You can find their pictures on the Internet.

If you, too, renounce being human, you can have a different job every day: doctor, movie star, astronaut, princess. *Princess* is a job in my world.

The best cars are pink. The best houses are pink.

If you let boys near you, they'll rip your clothes off, then your legs. Maybe your head.

I can stand up and walk with the help of a little girl. I guess I'm saying you should become a mother, just not to a boy. If you can help it.

Ken is nice, but I'm more interested in other women. Then again, I'm not sexual. That's for humans.

Everyone will bring you to life in a different way.

The less you speak, the more secrets people will tell you.

Jesus doesn't matter to me. I'll never die, I'll just get abandoned. My face will fade to dust in a basement.

My eyes never close. I look in mirrors when people make me.

Sometimes little girls can fix the damage little boys do. Sometimes not.

April

Tulips sprout all over in little brown boxes.
Sirens. Sirens make me think of rain
in the dark, red traffic lights blooming
on the pavement.

The yoga teacher says we probably feel torn up
because of the new sun and the tulips
and our anxiety. I've been trying to figure out
which I am:
a mountain, a warrior, a half-wheel who maybe wants
to be a wheel...

Each day I pass through a tunnel underground
to switch from one subway line
to the next. That's where I pray.
A New-York-Times-published poet
lives in the tunnel and pastes his poems
all over the walls. When he talks
he rocks his body back and forth,
arms crossed, and he wears a winter hat
even now.

People disappear for weeks
without notice. I give some art supplies
to the poet.

In the tunnel there is also a man selling incense
and a clown making balloon animals.
The man with a guitar smiles
as if he recognizes me.
I am the girl who often sings along.
But how could anyone recognize anyone
in a place like this?
A woman on the floor of the tunnel
with her child says *please*
and nothing else, the word stretching out
like a balloon being sculpted
into something else.

Spring is the end of winter,
which is where I have been living for years.
I lay down in the ice
and take some home to make a mess
so I can clean it up
and make another one.
The poet does not use the art supplies,
so I give them to the child
of the woman on the floor.
He draws me a picture
of a fish.

The yoga teacher says I can do a headstand
without leaning against anything—
stand upside-down in the middle
of any room. To me this sounds like saying
I can breathe underwater, make the dolphins
smile. Which I guess, technically,
I can.
I try the headstand,
and she is right.

The sun comes and goes. I always pick
the wrong jacket.

The sun can do whatever it wants
and, I realize suddenly, so can I.

Acknowledgements

"Letter of Complaint to a Dead Grandfather" and "Winter Landscape After Betrayal" originally appeared in *Tin House*.

"The Older Girl" originally appeared in *Booth*.

"A Mother Is a Vase Falling" originally appeared in *The Southern Review*.

"What My Father Said to Me This Morning" originally appeared in ZYZZYVA.

"Love Poem About My Internalized Homophobia, Which I Learned at Church" originally appeared in *Birdfeast*.

"Valentine's Day at the Psych Ward" and "When the Neighbors Get Evicted" originally appeared in *Figure 1*.

"Evening with Little Comfort" originally appeared in *New Ohio Review*.

"The Wedding Picture" originally appeared in *Spoon River Poetry Review*.

"April" originally appeared in BOAAT.

"Dream Poem About Matricide," "My Relationship with Beauty Will Always Be Conflicted," and "Blood Comes Like Rain After a Drought: Poem in Response to Your Shitty Poem" and "Smile" originally appeared in *Corresponding Voices*.

Caitlin Vance is a poet and fiction writer originally from Washington state. Her poems and stories have appeared in *Tin House, The Southern Review, ZYZZYVA, The Collagist, New Ohio Review, The Literary Review, Washington Square Review, Birdfeast, NightBlock, Figure 1*, and other magazines. Her poetry chapbook, *The Little Cloud*, was published by dancing girl press in 2018. She earned a BA in Philosophy from Colby College and an MFA in Creative Writing from Syracuse University. She is currently pursuing a PhD in English & Creative Writing at the University of Louisiana at Lafayette. Her academic interests include fairy tales, gothic literature, children's & young adult literature, and feminist theory & literary criticism. She is currently working on a middle-grade novel, a short story collection for adults, and a hybrid poetry project. Visit her website at caitlinmaryvance.com, or follow her on Instagram @caitlinmaryvance.

www.ingramcontent.com/pod-product-compliance
Lightning Source LLC
Chambersburg PA
CBHW030133100526
44591CB00009B/641